D0629484

CHRISTMAS GIFTS THAT ALWAYS FIT

Christmas Gifts That Always Fit

JAMES W. MOORE

DIMENSIONS
FOR LIVING

NASHVILLE

CHRISTMAS GIFTS THAT ALWAYS FIT

Copyright © 1996 by Dimensions for Living

This book is printed on recycled, acid-free paper.

Library of Congress Cataloging-in-Publication Data

Moore, James W. (James Wendell), 1938–
    Christmas gifts that always fit/James W. Moore.
      p.   cm.
    ISBN 0-687-06148-2 (hardcover: alk. paper)
    1. Christmas.   I. Title.
BV45.M64   1996
263'.91—dc20   96-19532

Unless otherwise noted Scripture quotations are from the New Revised Standard Version Bible, Copyright 1989 by the Division of Christian Education of the National Council of the Churches of Christ in the USA. Used by permission.

Those noted RSV are from the Revised Standard Version of the Bible, copyright 1946, 1952, 1971 by the Division of Christian Education of the National Council of the Churches of Christ in the USA. Used by permission.

In chapter 1, sections from *The Best Christmas Presents Are Wrapped in Heaven* by David Heller are copyright © 1993 by David Heller. Reprinted by permission of Villard Books, a division of Random House, Inc.

Howard Thurman's poem on p. 77 is from *The Mood of Christmas*, © 1973 Howard Thurman.

96 97 98 99 00 01 02 03 04 05 — 10 9 8 7 6 5 4 3 2 1

MANUFACTURED IN THE UNITED STATES OF AMERICA

For my family and loved ones,
who always make Christmas
so special, so joyous, so sacred

CONTENTS

❀

CHRISTMAS GIFTS THAT ALWAYS FIT

INTRODUCTION
Christmas Gifts That Always Fit

*F*rom the time the Magi brought gifts to the manger, Christmas has been a time of giving—gifts to those we love, gifts to the less fortunate, gifts to the church, gifts to various charities, gifts to family, gifts to friends, and even gifts to our pets.

A few Christmases ago, I was getting into the spirit of the season. I was "making a list and checking it twice" when I discovered that I needed another kind of list.

I needed a list of sizes. A size list is very important because so often we give gifts of clothing, and we want our gifts to fit. As I was working on my list, my mind drifted away from the practical task at hand, and I found myself thinking deeper thoughts, thoughts about the true meaning of Christmas and the very reason for our gift giving—thoughts about Christmas gifts that always fit.

Unfortunately, for many of us, Christmas has become little more than a time for purchasing and receiving gifts. We have become so focused on the material aspects of the season that we have lost sight of the Christmas gifts that always fit—the gifts that money can't buy.

What are those gifts? If you made your own list, what would be on it? As you think about that, try these on for size.

The Gift of Time

The gift of time is a Christmas gift that always fits. And in the hectic pace of Christmas, it may well be the most precious and most valuable gift we can give someone we love—a little slice of time, a little uninterrupted time just for that person!

"The greatest gift I ever received," said a respected and successful attorney, "was a gift I got one Christmas when my dad gave me a small box. Inside was a note: 'Son, this year I will give you 365 hours, an hour a day, every day after dinner. It's yours! We'll talk about what you want to talk about. We'll go where you want to go. Or we'll play what you want to play. It will be your hour! This is my gift to you this year, the gift of time!' My dad not only kept his promise, but that time together became so special to us that he renewed it every year. It's the greatest Christmas gift I ever received."

This raises an interesting question that we might want to consider each year at Christmas: Is there someone near us to whom we need to give a little more time?

* College students have come home for the holidays, wondering what to give their parents. What could be better than just a little slice of time, time just for them?
* High school students will be out of school for a few days, but still very, very busy with shopping and dates and Christmas programs and parties. Wouldn't it be nice if they could give just a little bit of time to mom and dad?
* Parents are rushing to and fro, coping with long lines, traffic jams, and heavy schedules; poring over checklists of things to be done, decorations to be arranged, trips to be planned, food to be cooked, gifts to be selected, toys to be bought, cards to be mailed, presents to be delivered, and bills to be paid. Wouldn't it be great, in the midst of all that chaos and confusion, to find a little uninterrupted and unhurried time for the children?
* Husbands, wives, grandparents, shut-ins, people who are sick or lonely or grieving — maybe the best thing to give them in this sacred season is a little

time. The gift of time is always appropriate, and it always fits.

The Gift of Kindness

At this time of year, our emotions are taxed a bit, and it is easy to become impatient and irritable. But it doesn't need to be that way. We don't need to be thoughtless or rude or edgy or harsh or hostile. We can be *kind!*

One of the most obvious signs of Christian faith is kindness. You can be an authority in theology, you can speak of the great philosophers, you can master church history, you can quote verses of scripture—but only when others see your kindness do they really begin to see your faith. John Boyle O'Reilly expressed it powerfully in rhyme:

> "What is real good?" I asked in musing mood;
> "Order," said the law court;
> "Knowledge," said the school;
> "Truth," said the wise man;
> "Pleasure," said the fool;
> "Affection," said the maiden;
> "Beauty," said the page;
> "Freedom," said the dreamer;
> "Home," said the sage;
> "Fame," said the soldier;
> "Equity," said the seer,
> But spake my heart full sadly,

"The answer is not here."
Then within my bosom, softly this I heard:
"Each heart holds the secret;
'Kindness' is the word!"

There's no question about it. This Christmas and every Christmas, there will be someone near us who, more than anything else, needs the gift of kindness. It's a gift that is always appropriate, a gift that money can't buy. It's a wonderful gift that always fits.

The Gift of Appreciation

I am convinced that people are hungry for appreciation. Some years ago, when Dr. William L. Stidger was at the Boston School of Theology, he sat down one day to write some notes of appreciation to people who, over the years, had touched his life in special ways and influenced his life for good. He remembered a favorite schoolteacher, a woman who taught English in secondary school and had gone out of her way to help him. She had kindled within him a burning hunger for knowledge. She had inspired him and taught him how to write. She had placed deep within him a love for literature. She had greatly influenced his life and the lives of countless other students.

A few days after he sent that former teacher a letter saying thanks, he received this reply:

My dear Willie, I cannot tell you how much your note meant to me. I am in my eighties now, living alone in a small room, cooking my own meals, lonely, and, like the last leaf of autumn, lingering behind. You will be interested to know that I taught school for fifty years, and yours is the first note of appreciation I have ever received. It came on a blue, cold morning, and it cheered me as nothing has in many years.

When Dr. Stidger read that note, he cried. As he thought of other people who had been kind to him, he remembered a bishop who had been most helpful at the beginning of his ministry. Now the bishop was in retirement and recently had lost his wife. Dr. Stidger sat down and wrote him a belated letter of thanks. Back came this reply:

My dear Will, your letter was so beautiful, so real, that as I sat reading it in my study, tears fell from my eyes—tears of gratitude. Then before I realized what I was doing, I rose from my chair and called my wife's name to show it to her—forgetting for a moment that she was gone. You will never know how much your letter has warmed my spirit. I have been walking about in the glow of it all day long. (W. E. Sangster, *Special Day Sermons* [Nashville: Abingdon Press, 1961]).

The gift of appreciation may be the most fitting gift that you and I could give someone this Christmas.

The Gift of Encouragement

In a wonderful verse in the book of Isaiah, the prophet announces that the Lord has given him "the tongue of a teacher," which enables him to "sustain the weary with a word" (50:4). Wouldn't it be great if all of us had the ability to encourage people when they are down, or tired, or low?

Bill Lufburrow, who was a good friend of mine, once told about an interesting Christmas experience he had some years before. At 9:45 in the evening, the front doorbell rang. When Bill opened the door, he found several children standing there, ranging in age from about six to ten.

One of them said proudly, "Hi! We're cheering up the neighborhood!" Then he said, "One, two, three," and they all yelled loudly, "Cheer! Cheer! Cheer!" And with that, they disappeared as quickly as they had arrived.

Isn't that great? Little children spreading cheer, cheering up the neighborhood; little children being the sons and daughters of encouragement.

On a silent and holy night a long time ago, encouragement came to the world as never before, through a little child, and when we really think about it, we too want to cheer, cheer, cheer! So what better gift could we give someone this Christmas than the gift of encouragement? It's a gift that is always appropriate. It's a gift that always fits!

The Gift of Love

The most important gift of all is the gift of love. It's so important, in fact, that we will come back to it again and again throughout the pages of this book. Love — that is precisely what Christmas is all about. What the people near us need this Christmas season more than anything else is the gift of love.

In the early 1500s, the great Protestant reformer Martin Luther was preaching a sermon on the Christmas story. Luther asked his congregation to meditate on the events surrounding the birth of Jesus, as if it were their own story; and then, rather vividly, he pictured Mary as being tired, cold, afraid — so young and having to be both mother and midwife. And he pictured Joseph nervously trying to help as best he could.

All of a sudden, Luther turned on his congregation. He had anticipated their reaction, and he said to them something like this: "I know what you are thinking. You are thinking, 'If only I had been there. How quick I would have been to help with the baby. I would have washed the linen. How happy I would have been to go with the shepherds to see the Christ Child, or bring a gift to the manger with the wise men.' Yes, you would say that because you now know how great Jesus is; but if you had been there at the time, you probably would have been no better than the people of Bethlehem! What childish and silly thoughts! But why don't you do it now? You have Christ in your neighbor, so why don't you serve your neighbor now? For what you do to your neighbor, you do to the Lord Jesus Christ himself!"

As the hymn writer so aptly put it: "Love came down at Christmas," and what could be more fitting than to receive that love, and then "pass it on" to others? Oscar Hammerstein expressed it so well:

> Love in your heart isn't put there to stay;
> Love isn't love 'til you give it away.

Time, kindness, appreciation, encouragement, love—these are only a few of the Christmas gifts that always fit. As we consider other timeless Christmas gifts and what they say to us about the greatest gift of all, the gift of God's Son, Jesus Christ, may we remember that the best gifts of all are free—freely given to us by God, for us to receive in faith and pass on to others. So my prayer is that we will reclaim the true meaning of Christmas this year by celebrating and giving the Christmas gifts that always fit!

1

The Best Christmas Presents
Are Wrapped in Heaven

"Be not afraid; for behold, I bring you good news of a great joy which will come to all the people; for to you is born this day in the city of David a Savior, who is Christ the Lord. And this will be a sign for you: you will find a babe wrapped in swaddling cloths and lying in a manger." Luke 2:10-12 RSV

few years ago, a Christmas present arrived at our home early in December. It was from a family of very special friends, and printed on the outside of the gift were those magical words that children of all ages love to see on a Christmas present: "Please Open Before Christmas!"

We tore into the present, and what we found was a wonderful book written by David and Elizabeth Heller — *The Best Christmas Presents Are Wrapped in Heaven: Children on Christmas*. And that is precisely what it is: children answering questions about Christmas. Children see some things in Christmas that we adults can so easily miss, as some of their thoughts and responses to these specific questions illustrate:

"What makes Christmas so special?"

Stacy (age 8): "Everything sparkles at Christmas . . . especially the people."

Johnny (age 7): "I like how the three kings brought presents, and that gave Santa Claus the big idea."

Russell (age 10): "Christmas is special [because] the birth of this child was a very important thing for this world."

Robbie (age 8): "The food is yummy! Stomachs love Christmas for that reason alone."

Marie (age 8): "Christmas [is special because] it makes everyone have a bigger heart."

Carey (age 7): "It gives you a chance to think about other people for a change."

Art (age 9): "Christmas is special because it is something you can count on every year . . . because it's created [by God] so it doesn't ever go away. It's forever!"

Victor (age 10): "Tis the season to have loving thoughts in your heart and Christmas cookies in your stomach."

Sylvia (age 10): "Christmas is special because 'Tis the season to be a child at heart.' "

"Why is Christmas good for families?"

Lem (age 10): "It shows you that you can be a happy family even if you live in a manger."

Gaye (age 9): "Christmas is the one day you can wake everybody up and get away with it."

And Brandi (age 10): "Christmas makes families say God Bless You even when nobody sneezes."

"What does the Christmas carol 'Silent Night' mean?"

Richard (age 9): "It means that peace is a good thing, and it might even be a holy thing of it lasts long enough."

Gaye (age 9): "It's supposed to be a quiet night because back there in the Holy Land, Jesus needed his sleep, to get ready to do all those miracles."

And Matthew (age 9): "When you see somebody special being born, you just get kind of amazed and quiet."

"What is the real message of Christmas?"

Henry (age 9): "The message is that wonderful things can happen here on earth too—but most of it starts higher up."

"What is the surest sign that Christmas is coming?"

Adam (age 8): "You hear people whistling 'Jingle Bells,' and nobody cares if they whistle good."
And Sylvia (age 10): "The biggest sign is one that we can't see. God is busier than before. He's working on what people really need for presents, [because, you see,] all the best Christmas presents are wrapped in heaven."

Sylvia is right, isn't she? The best Christmas presents are wrapped in heaven.

The Gospel writer John put it this way: "For God so loved the world that he gave his only Son, so that everyone who believes in him may not perish but may have eternal life" (3:16). Talk about a Christmas present! Talk about a gift that keeps on giving! Talk about a gift of love! This is the best Christmas present of all.

Luke tells about this amazing gift in his Christmas story:

In that region there were shepherds out in the field, keeping watch over their flock by night. And an angel of the Lord appeared to them, and the glory of the Lord shone around them, and they were filled with fear. And the angel said to them, "Be not afraid; for behold, I bring you good news of a great joy which will come to all the people; for to you is born this day in the city of David a Savior, who is Christ the Lord. And this will be a sign for you: you will find a babe wrapped in swaddling cloths and lying in a manger." And suddenly there was with the angel a multitude of the heavenly host praising God and saying, "Glory to God in the highest, and on earth peace among men with whom he is pleased!" (2:8-14 RSV)

The story tells us that the Christ Child was "wrapped in swaddling cloths and lying in a manger," but we know something deeper, don't we? Before that, this first and best Christmas present was wrapped in heaven.

That is God's Christmas gift for each of us. In the obscure form of a tiny baby born in a stable, the author of all life is saying: "Here, straight from heaven, this is the best I've got. Take this gift, receive this, embrace this. I give this gift to you because I love you so much."

This sacrificial gift from God is offered graciously and lovingly, but we need to do our part. We must accept it. We must receive it. We must treasure it. God won't force it on us. We need to reach out in faith and embrace and cherish and celebrate and receive into our hearts this amazing gift.

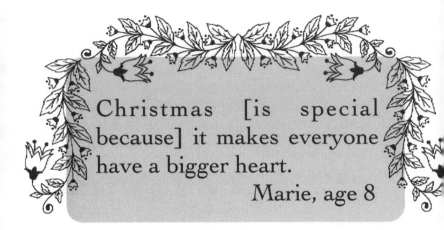

Christmas [is special because] it makes everyone have a bigger heart.

Marie, age 8

One of the greatest artists of all time was Pablo Picasso. After he was established as one of the world's great artists, everything Picasso did was worth a fortune.

One day he walked into a carpenter's shop to order a new piece of furniture for his home. He explained to the carpenter that he wanted a mahogany wardrobe that would fit in the corner of his bedroom.

The carpenter listened carefully, but appeared confused. A second time, Picasso described precisely what he wanted and how he wanted the wardrobe to look, but again the carpenter seemed unsure. Picasso tried a third time, but the carpenter still didn't seem to understand.

Finally, Picasso grabbed a pencil and a piece of scratch paper and sketched out precisely what he wanted.

"Oh yes, now I understand," said the carpenter.

"Well, how much?" Picasso asked.

"Nothing at all," the carpenter replied. "Just sign the sketch!"

The carpenter was a smart man. He knew that the best gift of all is that gift in which we give a part of ourselves. That's what God taught us at the first Christmas. When we give to others a portion of ourselves, that is a gift wrapped in heaven. Let's consider some of these gifts wrapped in heaven.

The Gift of Acceptance

In December 1993, the Bear Bryant Coach of the Year Award was presented to young Terry Bowden, the first-year coach at Auburn University. Terry had taken a struggling program that was on probation and led his team to an undefeated season.

Interestingly, Terry Bowden's father, Bobby Bowden, the coach at Florida State, also was nominated for the award. There was a lot of good-natured joking and teasing at the banquet about both father and son being considered for the same prestigious award. Of course, when Terry won, nobody in the room was happier or prouder than his dad.

In his acceptance speech, Terry thanked his team, his fellow coaches, Auburn University, and then his family.

"I owe so much to my parents," he said. "Many of you in this room know my mother, and you know how special she is, but let me tell you about my father.

"My parents always took us five kids to church. Even when we were on a trip, they took us to church. Once, while on vacation, we went to this church that was a little more emotional than we were used to. The minister was shouting and pounding the pulpit. He began to look around the congregation for someone to single out, and he spotted my father.

"Mom and Dad had marched us down to the front pew. Mom was on one end and Dad was on the other end, with the five kids squeezed in between, to be sure we would behave in church. The preacher pointed dramatically to my dad and this conversation took place:

"You there—do you have faith?"

"Yes, I have faith," Dad answered.

The preacher said: "If I put a 2x4 board down there on the floor, do you have enough faith to walk across it?"

"Yes, I could do that."

"But," said the preacher, "what if I took that same 2x4 board and placed it across the top of the two tallest buildings in New York City, would you have enough faith to walk across it then?"

"No, I don't have that much faith," Dad answered.

"But what if somebody were standing on the other end," said the preacher, "and was dangling one of your children off the side. Would you cross the board then?"

Terry said that his father turned and looked down the pew at his five kids and asked, "Which one?"

Of course, Terry was just kidding. The Bowdens are a very close-knit, loving family. But the point I want to make is this: Our Father God does not say, "Which one?" He doesn't say, "Which one should I lay my life on the line for?" God so loved the world that he wants to bring us all into the circle.

God comes with the open arms of acceptance for all of us. To each one of us, God says, "You are valued. You are included. You are wanted. You are precious to me."

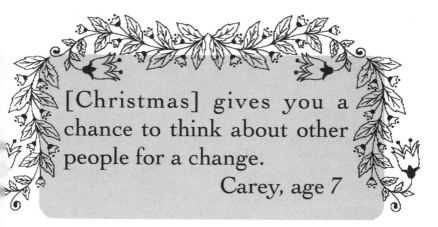

[Christmas] gives you a chance to think about other people for a change.

Carey, age 7

Now, we need to do our part. We need to accept God's acceptance. We need to receive this gracious gift. We need to welcome him into our hearts and lives with faith. And when we receive this Christmas present of acceptance offered to us by God, and live in that spirit, and pass the gift on to others, then we are giving them a Christmas present wrapped in heaven—the gift of acceptance.

If you want to give something special to someone at Christmas this year—to your children, your parents, your neighbors, your coworkers, your friends—just say to them, "You are valued. You are included. You are wanted and needed. You are precious to me." However you say it, you will give them a Christmas present wrapped in heaven—the gift of acceptance.

The Gift of Forgiveness

Steven Spielberg's movie *Schindler's List* is a graphic, shocking, unflinching depiction of the twentieth century's most staggering horror: the methodical, brutal extermination of millions of human beings in the Nazi death camps of World War II.

Oskar Schindler was a most unlikely hero. But through the efforts of this one man, some twelve hundred persons were saved from certain death. He put them to work in his factory, where he could protect them.

At one of the most powerful moments in the movie, Oskar Schindler is in conversation with the commander of the labor camp in Kraków, Poland. They are talking about power, and the commander (in his swaggering way) brags about the authority he has over these people. He says that when a man comes before him, he has the absolute authority to exterminate that man, if he so chooses. And he has been in the habit of doing just that—killing people brutally right and left, with no conscience at all.

But Oskar Schindler says, "Oh no, Commander, you are wrong. That is not power. Anyone could do that. But to have a man come before you and to say, 'I could take your life if I so choose, but no—instead, I pardon you!' That, Commander, is power!"

It is indeed the power of forgiveness, and that's the Christmas gift God offers us.

Martin Luther once became so frustrated with the evil he saw going on around him that he shouted, "If I were God and saw people acting the way they do, I would smash the world to bits!"

Luther might have, but not so with God. God comes into the world offering the gift of forgiveness: "I pardon you. I forgive you. I want to reclaim you."

That's the gift God offers, but we need to do our part. We have to accept the gift in faith. And when we accept forgiveness, and offer forgiveness to others, and live in the spirit of forgiveness, then we are doing a Godlike thing. We are offering a "Christmas present wrapped in heaven," the gift of forgiveness.

The Gift of Love

Love came down at Christmas. Robert Smith, of Stroudsburg, Pennsylvania, tells a true story that says it all: (Thanks to Don Shelby, December 24, 1992, "The Power of Love" sermon.)

It's been thirty years since I last saw her, but in memory she's still there every holiday season. I especially feel her presence when I receive my first Christmas card.

I was twelve years old and Christmas was only two days away. The season's first blanket of white magnified the excitement. I dressed hurriedly, for the snow was waiting. What would I do first — build a snowman, slide down the hill, or just throw flakes in the air and watch them flutter down?

Our family's station wagon pulled into the driveway, and Mom called me over to help with the groceries. When we finished carrying in the bags, she said: "Bob, here are Mrs. Hildebrandt's groceries."

No other instructions were necessary. As far back as I could remember, Mom shopped for Mrs. Hildebrandt's food and I delivered it. Our ninety-five-year-old neighbor who lived alone was crippled from arthritis and could take only a few steps with a cane.

Even though she was old, crippled, and didn't play baseball, I liked Mrs. Hildebrandt. I enjoyed talking with her; more accurately, I enjoyed listening to her. She told me wonderful stories about her life—about a steepled church in the woods and buggy rides on Sunday afternoons, and her family farm without electricity and running water.

She always gave me a dime for bringing in her groceries. It got so I would refuse only halfheartedly, knowing she would insist. Five minutes later, I'd be across the street in Bayer's Candy Store.

As I headed over with the grocery bags, I decided that this time would be different, though. I wouldn't accept any money. This would be my Christmas present to her. Impatiently, I rang the doorbell. Almost inaudible at first were the slow, weary shuffles of her feet and the slower thump of her cane. The chain on the door rattled, and the door creaked open. Two shiny eyes peered from the crack.

"Hello, Mrs. Hildebrant," I said. "It's me, Bob. I have your groceries."

"Oh yes, come in, come in," she said cheerfully. "Put the bag on the table."

I did so more hurriedly than usual, because I could almost hear the snow calling me back outside. She sat at the table, picked the items out of the bag, and told me where to set them on the shelves. I usually enjoyed doing this, but it was snowing.

As we continued, I began to realize how lonely she was. Her husband had died more than twenty years ago, she had no children, and her only living relative was a nephew in Philadelphia who never visited her.

Nobody ever called on her at Christmas. There would be no tree, no presents, no stocking. For her, Christmas was only a date on the calendar. She offered me a cup of tea, which she did every time I brought the groceries. Well, maybe the snow could wait.

Wonderful things can happen here on earth too—but most of it starts higher up.

Henry, age 9

We sat and talked about what Christmas was like when she was a child. Together, we traveled back in time, and an hour passed before I knew it.

"Well, Bob, you must be wanting to play outside in the snow," she said as she reached for her purse, fumbling for the right coin.

"No, Mrs. Hildebrandt, I can't take your money this time. You can use it for more important things," I resisted.

She looked at me and smiled. "What more important thing could I use this money for, if not to give it to a friend at Christmas?" she asked, and then placed a whole quarter in my hand.

I tried to give it back, but she would have none of it. I hurried out the door and ran over to Bayer's Candy Store with my fortune. I had no idea what to buy—comic books, chocolate soda, ice cream. But then, out of the corner of my eye, I spotted something. It was a Christmas card with an old country church in the woods on the front. It was just like the church Mrs. Hildebrandt described to me, and I knew I had to buy it.

I handed Mr. Bayer my quarter and borrowed a pen to sign my name.

"For your girlfriend?" Mr. Bayer asked.

I started to say "No," but quickly changed my mind. "Well, yes, I guess so."

As I walked back across the street with my gift, I was so proud of myself. I felt as if I had just hit a home run to win the World Series. No—I felt a lot better than that!

I rang Mrs. Hildebrandt's doorbell. The sounds of shuffling again reached my ears . . . the door cracked open.

"Hello, Mrs. Hildebrandt," I said as I handed her the card. "Merry Christmas to you!"

Her hands trembled as she slowly opened the envelope. She studied the card and began to cry.

"Thank you very much," she said in almost a whisper, "and Merry Christmas to you!"

On a cold and windy afternoon a few weeks later, the ambulance arrived next door. My mom said they had found Mrs. Hildebrandt in bed. She had died peacefully in her sleep. Her night-table light was still on when they found her, and it illuminated a solitary Christmas card, a card with an old country church in the woods on the cover.

The gifts of acceptance, forgiveness, love — these are some of the best Christmas presents of all, because they are the presents wrapped in heaven.

I'm Dreaming of a "Right" Christmas

*"Behold, a virgin shall conceive and bear a son,
and his name shall be called Emmanuel"
(which means, God with us).*

Matthew 1:23 RSV

A beautiful Christmas legend tells that one day God called the angels of heaven together for a special choir rehearsal. He told them there was a special song he wanted them to learn, a song they would sing at a very special occasion. The angels rehearsed long and hard, with great focus and intensity. In fact, some of them grumbled a bit, but God insisted on a very high standard for his choir.

As time passed, the choir improved in tone, rhythm, and quality, and finally God announced that they were ready. But then he shocked them a bit. He told them that they were to sing the song only once, and only on one night. There would be just one performance of this great song on which they had worked so diligently. Again, some of the angels grumbled: The song was so extraordinarily beautiful, and they had it "down pat" now. Surely they could sing it many, many times. But God only smiled and told them that when the time came, they would understand.

Then one night, God called them together. He gathered them above a field just outside of Bethlehem.

"It's time," God said to them, and the angels sang their song. Oh my, did they sing it: "Glory to God in the highest, on earth peace and good will toward all!" And as the angels sang, they knew that there never would be another night like this, that there never would be another birth like this birth in Bethlehem.

When the angels returned to heaven, God reminded them that they would not formally sing that song again as an angelic choir, but if they wanted to, they could hum the tune occasionally as individuals. One angel was bold enough to step forward and ask God why.

Why could they not sing that majestic anthem again? They did it so well. It felt so right. Why couldn't they sing that great song anymore?

"Because," God explained, "my son has been born, and now earth must do the singing!"

And once each year, Christmas comes around to remind us of that. "God's son has come to earth, and now we must do the singing!" And look at how we have tried! Without question, one of the best and most beloved parts of the celebration of Christmas is the music! The good news of Christmas is so awesome, so full of wonder, that it's not enough to just talk about it. We have to burst forth in song!

Think of it. There are the powerful anthems of Handel and Beethoven and Mozart and Rutter and Bach; the beloved carols — "O Little Town of Bethlehem," "Joy to the World," "The First Noel," "O Come All Ye Faithful," "Silent Night." Then there are the pop songs — "Jingle Bells," "Winter Wonderland," and "I'll Be Home for Christmas."

Once I was in a department store doing some Christmas shopping. Christmas music was playing, and I was getting into the spirit of it all, when suddenly I realized that I was singing along with Bing Crosby — "I'm dreaming of a white Christmas." Now, the chances of a "white Christmas" in my hometown of Houston are pretty remote — as they are in many parts of the country — but one thing we all can have is a "right Christmas."

"I'm Dreaming of a 'Right' Christmas." But how can that happen for us? How do we have a "right" Christmas? Let me suggest three things that need to happen.

We Need to Be Right with God

Getting right with God is the starting place, because that is indeed what Christmas is all about.

Jesus Christ came into this world to set us right with God.

Jesus Christ came into the world to save us and bring us back to God.

There is an old story about an elderly couple. They had the radio on one day as they drove through the busy streets, and as they listened to the beautiful music of Christmas, the wife became nostalgic:

"Herbert, do you remember when we were younger, we used to sit so close together as we drove along? It was so wonderful back then. What happened?"

"I don't know about that," said Herbert. "All I know is, I haven't moved!"

Well, Christmas comes each year to remind us that God is not the one who has moved away from us. No! We are the ones who have moved. We are the ones who have drifted away from him.

Some years ago, Dr. Hugh Litchfield told about taking his five-year-old son Christmas shopping one Saturday morning. It was just a day or so before Christmas, and the store was packed with shoppers. He told his son to stay near him, not to wander off, because he might so easily get lost in the crowd. After they had shopped together for awhile, Hugh was buying something for his wife at one of the counters. When he completed the purchase, he looked back, and his little five-year-old son was not there. He had drifted off!

So he began to search frantically. He called out, he rushed through the crowd, looking everywhere, but no luck! He moved quickly to the candy counter and then to the toy department (surely, he would be there) but no, he wasn't anywhere to be found.

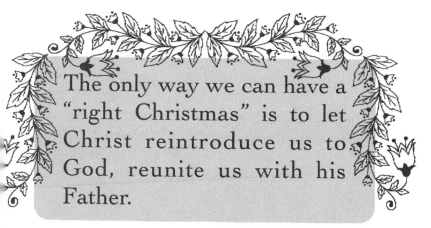

The only way we can have a "right Christmas" is to let Christ reintroduce us to God, reunite us with his Father.

Just as Hugh was about to panic, he suddenly heard this announcement over the department store loudspeaker: "We have a lost boy here! If you have lost your little boy, please come to the service desk!" Hugh hurriedly made his way there, and sure enough, there was his lost child. The reunion was a celebration, with lots of hugs and words of love, and visits to the candy counter and toy department. They had been apart, but they had found each other again! They had been brought back together.

The one who spoke over that loudspeaker, in a sense, served as a reconciler between the boy and his dad. They were lost from each other because the little boy had wandered off, drifted away, but the one at the service desk got them back together again. In the same sense, Christ has come down to this earth to help us get back together with the God who made us, the God who loves us. That's what that word *Emmanuel* means—God with us! God comes in the Christ Child to seek and save the lost. That's what Christmas is all about.

If we are to have a "right Christmas," we must let the Christ of Christmas bring us back to his Father who loves us, set us right with the One who made us. Every now and then, I see written on bumper stickers, plaques, and pins these words: "Jesus Is the Reason for the Season." Indeed so. The only way we can have a "right Christmas" is to let Christ reintroduce us to God, reunite us with his Father. The first step toward a "right Christmas" is to be set right with God.

We Need to Be Right with Ourselves

More and more psychologists are telling us that we can't feel good about life and other people until we feel good about ourselves. They call it a healthy self-esteem, which is simply another way of saying that we need to be right with our "selves."

Have you heard about the man who wrote this letter to the Internal Revenue Service?

> Dear Sirs: I underpaid my tax bill for last year. I can't sleep at night, and my conscience is bothering me. Enclosed please find $600.
> P.S. If I still can't sleep, I'll send the rest!

One of the best gifts we can give our loved ones . . . is to be at peace within.

A couple of years ago, Rick Pitino, head basketball coach at the University of Kentucky, suspended three of his star players. The reason: He had noticed them laughing and snickering as they watched the film of the previous Saturday's game. What was so funny? Silently, he studied the film and noticed that they were always laughing when one of the Kentucky players was shooting a free throw, a foul shot.

Suddenly he realized what they thought was so funny. They had tricked the referees and the other team by slipping someone to the foul line who had not been fouled. In other words, one player had been fouled, but another player (a better foul shooter) had slipped to the line to take the shots—a clear violation of the rules.

Coach Pitino said that the players thought it was all a big joke—that they had put something over on the officials and their opponents—but he didn't think it was a laughing matter. To make his point, he suspended three of his best players and made them sit out a very important conference game.

"They'll never do that again," said Coach Pitino, "and they'll never joke about that again. I want to win games for sure, but I also want my players to know the meaning of integrity."

Do you know the meaning of integrity, honesty, ethics, virtue, and morality? Do you feel good about your life right now, about who you are? We can be at peace with ourselves only when we welcome the Prince of Peace into our hearts and lives. We can be right with ourselves only when we are made right by him. One of the best gifts we can give our loved ones at Christmas this year is to be at peace within. If we are dreaming of a "right" Christmas, then first, we need to be right with God. And second, we need to be right with ourselves.

We Need to Be Right with Other People

I have a very special Christmas headband. It has mistletoe above it on a spring. When you wear it, everywhere you go, you are under the mistletoe. We have a friend in her eighties now who is so much fun. Two weeks before Christmas, she puts on her mistletoe headband and wears it everywhere. She "lights up" every place she goes, spreading Christmas joy with her beautiful radiance and her wonderful sense of humor. She is delightful, and she gets lots of kisses and hugs and smiles.

If you want to have a "right Christmas," go in the spirit of love and fix those broken relationships in your life.

Do you know where the custom of kissing under the mistletoe came from? Actually, it came from the Druids in northern Europe. They believed that mistletoe had curative power and could even cure separation between people. So when two enemies happened to meet under an oak tree with mistletoe hanging above them, they took it as a sign that they should drop their weapons and be reconciled.

When the missionaries moved in, they saw this mistletoe custom as a perfect symbol for what happened to the world at Christmas. At Christmas, a new age dawned—a time of peace, a time of healing, a time of reconciliation, a time for embracing one another.

If you want to have a "right Christmas," go in the spirit of love and fix those broken relationships in your life. If you are alienated, or estranged, or cut off, or at odds with any other person, go in the spirit of Christmas and make peace. Give the gift of peace. Don't put it off any longer. Drop your pride, drop your weapons, drop your grudges, and go set it right! Go, and God will go with you. That's what mistletoe is really about, and that's what Christmas is about. God comes to us in the Christ Child, so that we might be set right with God, set right with ourselves, and set right with other people.

3

The Best Things in Life
Aren't Things

And now faith, hope, and love abide, these three; and the greatest of these is love.   I Corinthians 13:13

ivian O'Guinn, an elementary schoolteacher, is the mother of seven children. Several years ago, she and ten friends and family members were enjoying an evening meal together. It was a pleasant event, with lots of joy and happiness around the table. After the meal, the children began playing dominoes. The adults innocently watched television.

Suddenly, there was a news flash about the city's massive rainfall and flooding. Then someone looked outside. Sims Bayou was rising, and the waters were moving slowly but surely toward the house. At about 9:30 in the evening, the water was coming through the walls. A call to the fire department brought advice: Unplug everything, pile up the mattresses, and put valuables on top.

Sims Bayou kept coming, and soon Vivian O'Guinn found herself standing with her children and friends on top of her son's new truck, as her refrigerator floated by. The snakes swimming around them convinced them not to try to wade to higher ground. Vivian realized suddenly that the following Sunday would be her birthday, and she found herself thinking and praying, "I'll never see that birthday. Oh, Lord, help us! We're not going to make it."

However, at 4:00 in the morning, a rescue boat arrived. It pulled right up to the truck roof on which they were standing, and carted all eleven people to safety. Except for her Bible and a few photo albums, Vivian O'Guinn lost everything, including her house. But later, she said to a reporter, "It's O.K. We lost all of our things, but things can be replaced. What matters is that we all were saved. We all got out safely. That's what counts. My children, my family, and my friends are all alive and well. We feel so blessed and so grateful." (*The Houston Post,* Nov. 24, 1994)

> When you are caught in a life-threatening situation, you quickly realize what is important, what matters, what counts—and that material things are fragile and undependable.

What Vivian O'Guinn was saying is that "the best things in life *aren't* things." She was saying that going through an experience like that, horrible as it was, will straighten out your priorities in a hurry. When you are caught in a life-threatening situation, you quickly realize what is important, what matters, what counts—and that material things are fragile and undependable.

In the Sermon on the Mount, Jesus put it dramatically: "Do not store up for yourselves treasures on earth, where moth and rust consume and where thieves break in and steal; but store up for yourselves treasures in heaven, where neither moth nor rust [nor flood] consumes and where thieves do not break in and steal. For where your treasure is, there your heart will be also" (Matt. 6:19-21).

Recently, I ran across an article that fascinated me. It was in *McCall's* magazine (January 1993) and was written by Linda Ellerbee, a noted television journalist. What caught my attention was the title the author had given her article: "The Five Best Things I Know." It's a listing of the five most valuable lessons Linda Ellerbee has learned during her extraordinary life:

1. Do what you believe is right.
2. In this world, a good time to laugh is any time you can.
3. Always set a place in life for the unexpected guest.
4. If you don't want to get old, don't mellow.
5. The best things in life really aren't things.

Linda Ellerbee says she learned that last one the hard way, when her teenage daughter ran away from home. Ms. Ellerbee concludes her article by saying that for her, the best things in life are health, love, friendship, and, most important, family.

That's a good list. What are the five most valuable lessons you've learned in your lifetime? What are the five best things you know? You and I might list things such as truth, honesty, integrity, morality, courage, commitment, church, grace, gratitude, goodness, compassion, forgiveness, kindness, salvation. There is no question about it—the best things in life *aren't* things.

The apostle Paul talks about this in one of his letters to the Corinthian Church. In that letter, he actually gives us his list of the best things in life. He starts out by saying (in effect): "Now, I know you have tried lots of different things—things like immorality and greed and materialism and cliques and idolatry. I know you have looked for happiness in lots of different places. I know you have experimented with this and that and the other. But now let me show you the higher gifts, the best things in life." And then he lists them for us: faith, hope, and love.

This Christmas, as we make our shopping lists and check them twice, as we fight our way through traffic jams and pray for patience as we stand in long lines, as we try to do all the many things we have to do to get ready for Christmas, and as we try to figure out how to get it all paid for, it just might help us to remember that the best things in life really are not things. They are, according to the Bible, faith, hope, and love. If you want to give something really special to your children or your parents, or to any other loved ones this Christmas, remember that there are no better gifts than these three.

The Gift of Faith

I imagine that almost every parent's nightmare on Christmas Eve is a box with these three words printed on top: SOME ASSEMBLY REQUIRED. Don Shelby tells this story about the father who had ordered a tree house for his children. When it was time to assemble the tree house, he laid out all the parts on the floor and began to read the instructions. To his dismay, he discovered that the instructions were for a tree house. However, the parts were for a sailboat!

The next day, he sent an angry letter to the company, complaining about the mix-up. Back came this reply: "We are truly sorry for the error and the inconvenience. However, it might help to consider the possibility that somewhere there is a man who is out on a lake trying to sail your tree house!"

The point is clear: To put something together, you must have the right parts and the right instructions. This is where faith comes in. The only way you can put life together is through faith. Faith in Jesus Christ, our Lord and Savior—that's what makes it work. That's the way to assemble your life—root it in Jesus Christ through faith, tie it to Jesus Christ, ground it in Jesus Christ.

Max Lucado, in *When God Whispers Your Name*, puts it dramatically and graphically:

Take a fish and place him on a beach. Watch his gills gasp and scales dry. Is he happy? No! How do you make him happy? Do you cover him with a mountain of cash? Do you get him a beach chair and sunglasses?

Do you bring him a "Playfish" magazine and a martini? Do you wardrobe him in double-breasted fins and people-skinned shoes? Of course not!

So, how do you make him happy? You put him back in his element. That's what you do. You put him back in the water. He will never be happy on the beach. Simply because he was not made for the beach. (Dallas: Word, Inc., 1993)

Indeed so, and the same is true for you and me. We will never be happy living apart from the One who made us. Just as a fish was made to live in water, we were made to live in close fellowship with God, and nothing can take the place of that.

This Christmas, you can give a child a polo shirt or a cashmere sweater or Cole-Hahn shoes or a Mercedes automobile, or a ski trip to Colorado, if you want to. But let me tell you something with all the feeling I have in my heart. The best gift you can give a child is Jesus Christ. If you want to do something good for the children in your life, if you want to give them the gift that keeps on giving, introduce them to Jesus Christ. Get them completely involved in his church. Show them how important your faith is to you. Give them the real gift of Christmas, the gift of the Christ Child. Help them discover the power of the Christian faith. Faith — it's one of the best things you can give them. It's one of the best things in life.

The Gift of Hope

Some years ago, a military airplane crashed at Sonderstrom Air Force Base in Greenland. Twenty-two people were killed. The runway and the nearby fields were strewn with bodies. It was a tragic and horrible moment. There was only one chaplain on the base at the time, and the entire burden was laid on him to bring comfort and the word of Christ to a shocked community staggered by the horrendous accident. But there was little time to mourn that day. The grisly task of gathering and identifying the bodies was still to be done.

And so the chaplain, along with a young lieutenant who had been assigned the duties of mortuary officer, and a group of volunteers, went about the awful business of picking up the mutilated bodies and trying to identify the dead, so that their loved ones back home could be notified. It was a heartbreaking and exhausting task, and the people worked in shocked silence well into the night, until they almost dropped from fatigue.

When every last remnant of death had been recovered, they each went silently to their individual rooms. That night, after midnight, there was a knock on the chaplain's door. Outside stood the young lieutenant, the mortuary officer. He said nothing. He just stood there and wept. After some moments, he spoke through his tears:

"As we were picking up the bodies today, I realized something. I realized that the only other people out there with us were the people who go to church here. I have always been an unbeliever, and I used to ridicule these same people who were out there with us. Yet they are the only persons who would, or perhaps could, do what we had to do today. It must have been their Christian spirit that could help them see beyond the horror to the hope."

Once each year, Christmas comes along to renew our hope and to remind us that the darkness of this world cannot overcome the light of our Lord.

That tragic day turned the life of that young lieutenant around. As he had admitted, he had never been religious, had seldom gone to church except for weddings and funerals, but from that time on, he was a new man. Christ was born in his heart, and he took an active part in the Christian ministry of that base. Then he did an unheard of thing: The first person on that base to do so, he extended his tour of duty in Greenland for an extra year. He did it because he wanted to be able to tell others how the power of Christian hope had changed his life. (Edward Beckstrom, "The Wind of the Spirit," *Minister's Annual 1988* [Nashville: Abingdon Press])

If you want to give your loved ones a great Christmas present this year, give them the hope of the Christian faith. On page after page of the New Testament, we find it—the good news that God will win, that nothing can defeat God. Ultimately, God and goodness will be victorious, and when we have faith in God, nothing (not even death) can separate us from God's care, God's love, and God's triumph. Once each year, Christmas comes along to renew our hope and to remind us that the darkness of this world cannot overcome the light of our Lord.

The Gift of Love

During World War II, four young American soldiers who had been in battle for some time were sent back from the front lines to a small French village for a little "R&R." When they arrived in the village, they suddenly realized that it was Christmas Eve, and they began to discuss how they would spend Christmas.

The soldier went over to the little girl and gently said, "What do you want most for Christmas?" And the little girl said, "I want somebody to hold me."

One of the soldiers said, "You know, as we were coming into town earlier today, I noticed an orphanage on the outskirts of the village. Why don't we go there in the morning and take some Christmas joy to those children?"

The others liked the idea, and the more they talked about it, the more excited they became. So they went out and bought all kinds of toys and candy and clothing and food and books and games, and early the next morning, they showed up at the front door of the orphanage with wonderful Christmas presents for all the children. The orphanage director was pleased, and all the children were delighted as they opened their gifts — all the children, that is, except one little girl, who stood quietly off to the side. She appeared to be five or six years old, and she looked so very sad.

One of the American soldiers noticed that the little girl was not participating, and he asked the orphanage director about her.

"Oh, bless her heart," said the director. "We just got her last week. Both of her parents were killed in a car wreck. There was no one to take her in, so we brought her here."

The soldier went over to the little girl and gently said, "It's Christmas morning, and we have wonderful Christmas presents here — toys, clothes, candy, food, books, puzzles. Which would you like? What do you want most for Christmas?"

And the little girl said, "I want somebody to hold me."

Maybe that is the best Christmas gift of all — someone to hold us. As a wise person once said, "Rich is not *what* you have. It's *who* you have beside you." This sacred season comes along once each year to remind us that "Love Came Down at Christmas," that even now, God is reaching out to us with open arms. And God wants us to accept his love and pass it on to others.

Faith, hope, and love are not only the best Christmas gifts. They are the best things in life!

4

Precious Gifts of Gold, Circumstance, and Mud

Then, opening their treasure chests, they offered him gifts of gold, frankincense, and myrrh.   Matthew 2:11*b*

*O*ne of the most charming stories I have ever read was written by Rex Knowles, whose wife went Christmas shopping one Saturday afternoon and left dad home to baby-sit.

The father was enjoying the quiet time at home, reclining on the couch in the den, half-dozing and half-watching a college football game.

Suddenly, the children disturbed his peace by announcing loudly: "Daddy, Daddy, we have a play to put on. Do you want to see it?"

Daddy didn't, especially, but he knew he would have to; so he went into the living room and sat down, a one-man audience. He saw quickly that it was a Christmas play.

At one end of the piano bench was a flashlight. It was turned on, wrapped in "swaddling clothes," and lying in a shoebox.

Then Rex (age six) came in, wearing Dad's bathrobe and carrying a mop handle. He was followed by Nancy (age ten), who announced: "I'm Mary, and this is Joseph." Then Trudy (age four) entered with pillowcases over her arms, which she waved about, saying, "I am an angel."

Finally, in came Anne (age eight), riding a camel. At least, she moved as though she were riding a camel, because she had on her mother's high-heeled shoes. She was bedecked with all the jewelry available and carried a pillow, on which rested three Christmas presents.

She went over, bowed before the "Holy Family," and announced: "I am all three wise men. I bring precious gifts of gold, circumstance, and mud!" (*Guideposts*, December 1961, pp. 12-13)

That was all. The play was over. But Daddy did not laugh. He didn't correct his daughter. Rather, he prayed, because he realized how near his little daughter had come to the truth of Christmas. Of course, she had meant to say, "gold, frankincense, and myrrh," but even as she mixed up the words, she had got right to the heart of Christmas.

She had underscored the message of Christmas, because Christmas reminds us that we can indeed bring to God our gold, our circumstances—and yes, even our mud!

Christmas Reminds Us that We Can Bring Our Gold to God

Over the years, gold has come to symbolize our very best possessions, our substance, our material value. From the time of the wise men, Christmas has been a time for giving our best to God.

Every year at Christmas, my mind darts back to a television program I saw in 1960. Perhaps you remember the old show called *I've Got a Secret.* Gary Moore was the host. People would come on with unusual secrets, and a panel of celebrities would ask them questions and try to guess their secrets. The particular program I'm recalling now is something of a parable for the way we sometimes celebrate Christmas.

A group of people in Ohio decided to give a man a surprise birthday party. They got together and organized the party in great detail. They set up several committees to take care of the arrangements for food and entertainment and decorations.

There was a great hustle and bustle of excitement as they made ready for the big event. Finally, the evening of the party arrived, and all was in readiness. The hall was rented, the decorations were in place (they were outstanding), the food was prepared (it looked sumptuous), the entertainment was rehearsed and ready, the guests were there, the lights and sound were set to perfection.

Then suddenly, they realized something. Everything had been taken care of in splendid fashion, except one thing. They had forgotten the single most important thing. They had forgotten to invite the guest of honor! So they had the party without him. The man's secret was that he had not been invited to his own birthday party! Isn't that a poignant parable for us at Christmas?

Do we sometimes forget what it's really all about? Do we sometimes leave out the single most important thing? Do we sometimes fail to include the one whose birthday we are celebrating? Do we sometimes leave Christ and his church off our Christmas gift list?

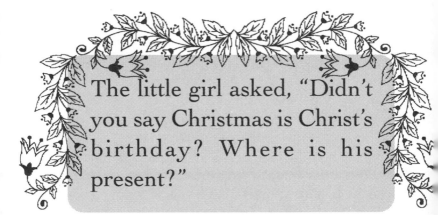

The little girl asked, "Didn't you say Christmas is Christ's birthday? Where is his present?"

Some years ago, I heard Dr. D. L. Dykes tell a beautiful story called "Where's His?" that makes the point so well:.

Once upon a time on a Christmas Eve night not long ago, a lady (who was not rich or poor), but whom God had blessed with a comfortable life and a comfortable family, was showing a little girl her Christmas tree.

The little girl said "What's Christmas?"

The lady answered, "Why, child, don't you know? Christmas is Christ's birthday, and this is the tree, and these are the Christmas presents. The red one over there is a hunting jacket for my husband. The big brown package is a television game for my granddaughter. The green one there is a calculator for my son. The striped one is a blouse for my niece."

And so on, over the huge pile of presents, the lady named them off for the little girl. When she finished, the little girl was silent as she looked over all the presents. Then she said quietly, "Where's His?"

"What do you mean?" asked the lady. "Have I forgotten someone? I've gone over that list so many times, who have I forgotten?"

The little girl asked, "Didn't you say Christmas is Christ's birthday? Where is his present?"

Christmas reminds us that we, like the wise men, can bring our gold to the Christ Child and his church. We can put Christ and his church on our gift list.

Christmas Reminds Us that We Can Bring Our Circumstances to God

We can bring to God our joys and sorrows, our victories and defeats, our biggest concerns and our smallest worries.

A couple of years ago while on a speaking engagement, I had breakfast with Jimmy, an old college classmate. He heard that I was in town and took me to breakfast. I learned that he is now a sales representative for a large national company.

During our visit, Jimmy told me about a recent experience he had with his new sales manager. He was driving his new boss around town when they happened to pass near Jimmy's home. Jimmy asked the new sales manager if he would like to stop by his house and meet his family. "My wife is baking an apple pie," Jimmy said, "and the children will just be coming in from school. Would you like to drop in?"

Jimmy was stunned by the new sales manager's irate and hostile reply: "Let's get one thing straight right now! I'm not interested in your family. I'm not interested in your wife or your children. I'm not interested in you personally at all, or any of the circumstances of

your life. All I'm interested in are results. All I'm
interested in about you is your sales record!"

God is with us in every
circumstance of life . . . and
nothing, not even death, can
separate us from God and
God's love.

Jimmy said, "That really hurt. I felt as though
someone had slapped me across the face, but you
know, I realized something. I realized that God is
the opposite of that! God *is* interested in my home
and my family. God *is* interested in my wife and my
children. God does care about me personally. He is
interested in all of the circumstances of my life."

That's the "good news of Christmas"—that
God cares and that God is with us. The word of
Christmas is "Emmanuel," which means "God
with us." God is with us in every circumstance

of life — indeed, even beyond this life — and nothing, not even death, can separate us from God and God's love.

We can bring our gold to the manger. And we also can bring our joys and sorrows to the Christ Child. We can give God our gold. And we also can give God our circumstances.

Christmas Reminds Us that We Can Bring Even Our Mud to God!

We can even bring our "mud" to the manger — our weaknesses, our failures, our foibles, our mistakes, our inadequacies, our sins — and somehow God, through the miracle of God's grace, can redeem them and reshape them.

Some time ago, I was working late in my office. Everyone else had gone home for the day. I was at my desk when I felt someone looking at me. Have you ever had that experience? I felt the presence of another person, and looking up, I saw standing at the doorway a young woman who looked to be in her early twenties. She was crying softly.

She said, "You don't know me, and I'm not a member of this church, but I need desperately to tell someone my story. Let me tell you what a terrible thing I've done, and then I want to ask you one question."

Through tears, her story unfolded. She had married at eighteen. The marriage lasted two years. Her husband deserted her. Hurt, scared, and confused, she wallowed for a time in self-pity, but then she became so lonely and so disoriented that she took up a lifestyle that was the total opposite of every moral value she had been taught—a lifestyle so sordid that she couldn't even look at me as she described it.

Earlier that evening, as she was driving through the streets of the city, she had seen the steeple of our church, and suddenly she was jolted by the reality of what her life had become. It hit her; it all caved in on her. As she thought back over the last few weeks and what she had been doing, she was ashamed, sorry, penitent.

She pulled into our church parking lot at that very moment, came to my office, and told me her story. She was obviously penitent.

Then came her question: "How could God ever forgive me for what I've done?"

I answered, "God already forgives you. The question is, Can you forgive yourself? Can you, in faith, accept God's forgiveness? Can you learn from this? Can you make a new start with your life?"

She still seemed unsure of God's forgiveness, so I went on, "Let me ask you to do something. I want you to imagine that you are my daughter and that you just told me your story exactly as you told it before. As a father, I would have two choices. I could say, 'Get out of my sight! You have dishonored our family! I disown you! Get out!' Or I could reach out to you with compassion and say, 'Oh, I am so sorry this has happened. I love you, and I want to help you! Let me help you make a new beginning with your life!'"

Then I asked her, "Now, which one of those do you think I would do?"

She said, "I think you would do the second."

"Why do you think that?" I asked.

"Because," she said, "even though I don't know you too well, I do know that you are a father and that you love your children!"

"Precisely!" I said to her. "And if I am capable of that kind of love and forgiveness, how much more capable of that is God!"

That's what Christmas is about. Christ comes to show us that God is a loving Father, not a vindictive judge who must be appeased. God is a gracious, merciful, loving Father, to whom, in faith, we can bring our gold, our circumstances, and even our mud. And God can take those gifts and redeem them, reshape them, and use them for good. That is the good news of Christmas!

What Can We Give the Christ Child for Christmas This Year?

When they saw the star, they rejoiced exceedingly with great joy; and going into the house they saw the child with Mary his mother, and they fell down and worshiped him.　　Matthew 2:10-11a RSV

ne of the most beloved legends of Christmas is the story of "The Little Drummer Boy." When the Christ Child was born, according to this story, many beautiful gifts were brought to the manger, gifts of great beauty and splendor. But one small boy was very poor, and he had nothing to offer the Lord. This made him very sad. But then he thought, "I know what I can do, I can play my drum for him."

And so he did—"Pa rum pum pum pum, Pa rum pum pum pum." He played with all the love in his heart. And as he played, so the legend tells us, the Christ Child smiled, showing that at Christmas, the gift of love is the best gift of all.

You see, it was not so much what the drummer boy did as how and why he did it. The real key was not his drum playing. I'm sure there were better drummers around. It was his spirit, his attitude of love, his desire to celebrate, his willingness to give of himself—those were the things that made the Christ Child smile. And they still do!

Each year at Christmas, we all pore over our gift lists, giving much time, effort, and energy to selecting just the right gifts to give to those we love—and that's fine. I'm all for it, especially if the gift giving is a part of our faith response to the greatest Christmas gift of all: God's gift of the Savior to the world, God's gift of the Christ Child to you and me.

But as I have been mulling over this whole business of gift giving at Christmas, my mind keeps drifting back to the images of the Little Drummer Boy and the wise men bringing their gifts to the Christ Child at the manger. And I have found myself grappling with this question: What can we give to the Christ Child for Christmas this year? What are the best gifts you and I can bring to the manger? What can we give him?

In 1872, Christina Rossetti wrote a beautiful poem with these poignant words:

> What can I give Him,
> Poor as I am?
> If I were a shepherd,
> I would give Him a lamb;
> If I were a Wise Man,
> I would do my part, —
> But what I can I give Him,
> I give my heart.

With this as a backdrop for our thinking of the many appropriate gifts that each of us might give to the Christ Child this year, let me suggest three.

We Can Bring the Christ Child Our Penitence

We should start with penitence, sorrow for our sins. This is what the Advent and Christmas seasons underscore for us so dramatically—how much we need a Savior! This world is not enough. Apart from God, we are incomplete. We have sinned. We can't make it by ourselves. We need help. We need a Savior.

When a young man filled out an application for admission to college, one of the questions asked: "What are your personal strengths?"

The young man wrote: "Sometimes I'm trustworthy, loyal, cooperative, and kind."

Then the form instructed: "List your weaknesses," and he wrote: "Sometimes I'm not trustworthy, loyal, cooperative, or kind."

We can all relate to that, can't we? And that's why we approach the manger of Christmas on our knees in the spirit of penitence.

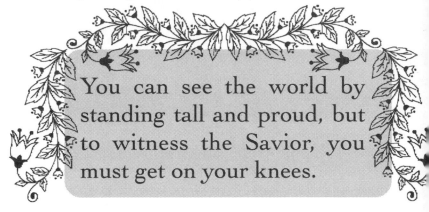

You can see the world by standing tall and proud, but to witness the Savior, you must get on your knees.

Have you ever been to the city of Bethlehem? A small cathedral there marks the supposed birthplace of Jesus. Behind the high altar in the church is a small cave lighted by silver lamps. You can enter the quiet cave, where a star is embedded in the floor to mark the spot of the manger on that first Christmas night.

You can come to that sacred spot, but there is one stipulation. You must stoop to go in. The door is so low that you can't go in standing up. You can see the world by standing tall and proud, but to witness the Savior, you must get on your knees. You come in humility and penitence.

In *The Applause of Heaven,* Max Lucado puts it like this:

So . . .
   while the theologians were sleeping
      and the elite were dreaming
         and the successful were snoring,
            the meek [and penitent] were kneeling.
They were kneeling before the One only the meek [and penitent] will see. They were kneeling in front of Jesus.

(Dallas: Word Publishing, 1990, p. 73)

Some years ago, Bret Harte wrote *The Luck of Roaring Camp,* a powerful story that is a fascinating parable for Christmas. Roaring Camp was the meanest mining town in the west. It had more murders, fights, thefts, and drunkenness than any other town. It was a terrible place, inhabited entirely by tough miners. The only woman there was Cherokee Sal, and she died while giving birth to a baby.

The baby survived and was quite healthy. The miners thought, "What in the world are we going to do with a baby?" They put the baby in a box with some old rags, but they realized quickly that that wouldn't work. The box was not good enough or clean enough to hold the baby. So one of the men went to the next town, 80 miles away, to buy a cradle. He brought back a beautiful rosewood cradle, and they put the baby in it. But now the rags didn't look quite right.

So another man went to Sacramento and brought back some beautiful silk and lace blankets. They wrapped the baby in the new blankets and placed it in the new cradle, and then they noticed that the floor was filthy. So they got down on their hands and knees to clean the floor. That, of course, made the walls and ceiling and the dirty windows look terrible. So they washed the walls and the ceiling and put up some nice curtains. And now things were much better.

But of course, the men had to stop fighting, because they knew that would wake the baby. And soon the whole temperament of Roaring Camp seemed to change. Each day they took the baby to the mine entrance so everyone could look at the baby and see how it was growing. But they noticed that the entrance of the mine was unattractive, so they planted a beautiful garden there.

The miners liked to touch the baby and pat its hand, but their hands looked so dirty next to the baby. Well, pretty soon the general store had sold out of soap, and before long, life in Roaring Camp had completely changed. The men had given up their hostile, profane ways — all for the love of a baby!

Yes, the redemptive, life-changing power of a baby — that's the good news of Christmas. We can bring to the Christ Child our penitence, and he will exchange gifts with us. He will take our sins and give us the gift of salvation and life.

We Can Bring the Christ Child Our Commitment

What better gift could we give to the Christ Child this Christmas than the gift of commitment — to commit ourselves, body, mind, and spirit to him, to his church and to his cause?

There is a story about a man who went into the bus station in Athens, Georgia, to buy a ticket to Greenville, South Carolina. The ticket clerk told him that the bus would be a little late. While he was waiting, he thought he'd walk around and take a look at things. As he explored the bus terminal, he came upon a machine which advertised that for 25¢, "I will tell you your name, your age, your hometown, and other interesting information."

Curious and somewhat skeptical, the man took out a quarter and put it into the machine. A card came out of the slot: "Your name is Bill Jones. You are 35 years of age. You live in Athens, Georgia. You are waiting for a bus to Greenville, South Carolina. The bus is delayed." The man was dumbfounded. The machine did exactly what it said it would do! How could it do that? He was amazed.

He decided to try it again. He put in another quarter, and another card came out: "As I told you before, your name is Bill Jones. You are 35 years old. You live in Athens, Georgia. You are still waiting for a bus to Greenville, South Carolina. The bus is delayed a little longer."

Many people . . . spend all their time and energy horsing around, and they miss the bus. They never get on the bus; they never make a commitment.

It was just incredible. Now, he was really fascinated. He thought, "I'm going to stump this machine." He ran across the street to a dime store and bought one of those Groucho-Marx disguises—the glasses with thick eyebrows and mustache. He also bought some fake ears, a wig, and a cane. Then he hobbled back to the station, approached the machine, and inserted a quarter.

Out came the card: "Well, it's you again. Your name is still Bill Jones. You are 35 years old. You live in

Athens, Georgia. You want to go to Greenville, South Carolina. But the problem is that while you were horsing around, you missed your bus!"

Many people are like that. They spend all their time and energy horsing around, and they miss the bus. They never get on the bus; they never make a commitment. One of the best gifts we can give the Christ Child for Christmas this year is our unflinching, unwavering commitment, a commitment that will boldly take up the torch of his ministry, hold it high, and carry it forward.

Are you really committed to Christ, with all your heart and soul? Are you as committed to Christ as you want to be, or as you ought to be? Are you really and truly on the bus? Or are you just horsing around the station?

On a Christmas card our family received, one writer expressed it like this:

When the song of the angels is stilled,
When the star in the sky is gone,
When the Kings and princes are back home,
When the shepherds have returned to their flocks,
The work of Christmas begins;
To find the lost, To heal the broken,
To feed the hungry, To release the prisoners,
To rebuild the nations, To bring Peace among people,
To make music in the heart.
[Or, in other words, to do the work of Christ!]
(Howard Thurman, Fellowship of Reconciliation, Nyack, N.Y.)

When we do the work of Christ, we give the gift of commitment. What a fitting and beautiful gift to bring to the manger!

We Can Bring the Christ Child
Our Love for Others

At first hearing, this sounds like a strange gift to give the Christ Child: "One of the best gifts we can give the Christ Child for Christmas this year is our love for others"? Yet that's what he wants most of all. Remember how he said it: "As you did it to one of the least of these . . . you did it to me" (Matt. 25:40).

I am convinced that nothing in this world touches the heart of Christ and makes it glad more than when he sees us love one another, care for one another, be kind to one another. I'm equally convinced that nothing in this world breaks the heart of Christ more than when he sees us hurt one another.

Someone once said that necessity is the mother of invention. This was certainly true for one family back during the Great Depression. The mother, the father, and the six-year-old son, Pete, had absolutely no money one Christmas for store-bought presents, but that didn't keep them from giving and celebrating Christmas.

They decided to make pictures of the presents they would like to give one another, if money were no object. They couldn't afford the real gifts, so they drew pictures, or cut pictures out of catalogs and magazines of what they would most want to give the others if they could. Then they put the pictures in old boxes left over from prior Christmases, stuck some old bows on them, and placed them under the tree.

And on Christmas morning, never was a tree heaped with such riches. The gifts were only pictures, to be sure, but they were symbols of Christmas giving. There was a shiny new car for Dad and a red motor boat, some golf clubs, a new suit, some sweaters, and an all-weather coat.

When Mom opened her "play-like" gifts, she found her dream house and a diamond necklace, dresses and coats and shoes, a new silver service, and a vacation cruise.

However, most of the make-believe picture gifts were for little Pete. They were pictures of wonderful gifts—a fabulous camping tent, a bicycle, a pedal car, all kinds of games and sports equipment, even a back-yard swimming pool.

They had a great time opening their imaginary presents. Now, of course, Mom and Dad didn't expect any "best present" from Pete. After all, he was only six.

But finally, with squeals of delight, he crawled under the Christmas tree and pulled out a gift he had prepared and hidden way back in the corner. With a big smile, Pete handed the present to his folks, and when his mom and dad opened it, they found a picture he had drawn with his first-grade crayons.

He had used bright flashy colors and a modernistic drawing technique. But it was unmistakably the picture of three people laughing—a man, a woman, and a little boy.

> In a simple crayon drawing, six-year-old Pete had reminded them that cars and boats and clothes and toys may be nice, but love for one another is the best gift of all.

They were standing side by side, with their arms around one another. They were warmly united, connected, bonded. And it was obvious that they were radiantly happy together. Under the picture, Pete had printed just one word—"US." (Pleasantville, N.Y.: Reader's Digest Assn. [Margery Alcott, "The Christmas We Will Never Forget"], *Reader's Digest*, 1959)

Mom and Dad looked at that picture through tears of joy, because they realized that in the years to come, they would receive lots of Christmas presents, but they knew they would never receive a better Christmas gift than this one! In a simple crayon drawing, six-year-old Pete had reminded them that cars and boats and clothes and toys may be nice, but love for one another is the best gift of all.

Penitence, commitment, and love for one another. These are great Christmas gifts to bring to the manger. They are gifts of the heart—great gifts to give to the Christ Child for Christmas this year.

6
Bethlehem? Or Bedlam?

The angel said to them, "Be not afraid; for behold, I bring you good news of a great joy which will come to all the people."

Luke 2:10 RSV

*L*et's just go ahead and admit it! Christmas, for many people, is uproar, busyness, and wild confusion. Frayed nerves, emotional tensions, physical exhaustion, unpaid bills, long lines, traffic jams, difficult decisions, hectic schedules — all combine to make the Christmas season a time of busy confusion for many people. How many times during the season we hear people say, "If we can just get through Christmas!"

On the day before Christmas, one family was at its wit's end. The father was worn to a frazzle from too much walking and too many bills. The mother was on the verge of a nervous breakdown. Their little girl felt that she was "in the way." They had fussed at her and at each other all day long.

We can almost understand why, with the frustrations of the day weighing down upon her, that the little girl got her words mixed up in her bedtime prayer: "Give us this day our daily bread and forgive us our Christmases, as we forgive those who Christmas against us."

Christmas? or confusion? Bethlehem? or Bedlam? Which will you choose this year?

The truth is that we don't have to choose, because Christmas always happens right in the midst of our confusion. God breaks into our confusion and makes himself known! Bethlehem always comes in the midst of bedlam.

Christmas and confusion! Weren't they intimately related at the first Christmas when Jesus was born? Sometimes we forget that. Remember the bedlam in Bethlehem that night? Talk about confusion! Just think of it:

* a crowded inn,
* a stable,
* a census,
* political intrigue,

* soldiers marching in the street,
* a busy city, pushing and shoving,
* people scrambling for shelter.

In that confusion, Christmas happened! Christmas broke through! In that busy, hectic uproar, it happened, and those with the eyes and ears and hearts of faith saw it, heard it, felt it!

A Christmas card I received from a college student had been mailed during her exam week, a busy, frantic time. On the back of the envelope, she had hurriedly scribbled a poem:

> I longed to be alone with God
> To thank Him for His grace
> And have a quiet, peaceful talk
> In some secluded place.
> But yet confronting me each day
> Were tasks I could not shirk.
> "You just go right ahead," said God,
> "We'll visit while we work!"

This, you see, is the good news of Christmas: God meets us where we are! *He breaks into our uproar,* our busyness, our hectic pace, our darkness, our confusion, *and makes himself known as the King of kings,* the Light of the World, the gracious, forgiving God who understands.

Every now and then, the real spirit of Christmas breaks through the fog, the bedlam, the confusion, and clears things up—and that's what keeps us going.

Out in the country they have a saying: "Every now and then a blind squirrel finds an acorn." That old saying is simply a reminder that

* every now and then good things happen,
* every now and then we run into a pleasant surprise,
* every now and then things come into focus for us.

Well, Christmas happens every now and then. Every now and then, the real spirit of Christmas breaks through the fog, the bedlam, the confusion, and clears things up—and that's what keeps us going.

Every Now and Then, Christmas Breaks Through and Clears Up Our Confusion About God and What God Is Like

Christmas clears up our theological confusion. Christmas gives us a new picture of God, and what it reveals is "good news" and "glad tidings."

There is a story about a little seven-year-old boy who had been playing outside. His mother called him for dinner. The little boy ran in, jumped into his chair, and grabbed his fork, ready to eat.

"Wait, Tommy," said his mom, "you have germs on your hands. Go wash up before we eat." Tommy scrambled down, ran and washed his hands, came back, climbed up into his chair, grabbed his fork, and started to eat.

But again his mother stopped him. "Wait, Tommy," she said, "we must say the blessing before we eat. We want to thank God for our food."

Little Tommy put his fork down, mournfully shook his head, and muttered wearily, "Germs and God, germs and God—that's all I ever hear around here, and I ain't never seen neither one of them!"

Now, we can sympathize with Tommy's predicament, but Christmas does help us here, because Christmas gives God a face. Christmas shows us who God is and what God is like.

William Barclay, in his *Commentary on Matthew*, put it like this:

> Jesus is the one person who can tell us what God is like, and what God means us to be. In Jesus alone we see what God is like, and we see what man ought to be like. Before Jesus came, men had only vague and shadowy, and often quite wrong, ideas about God; they could only at best guess and grope; but Jesus could say, "He that hath seen Me hath seen the Father" (John 14:9). In Jesus we see the love, the compassion, the mercy, the seeking heart, the purity of God as nowhere else in all this world. With the coming of Jesus the time of guessing is gone, and the time of certainty is come. . . . Jesus came to tell us the truth about God and the truth about ourselves.
>
> (Philadelphia: Westminster Press, 1956, Vol. I, p. 11)

This, you see, is the "good news" of Christmas. Jesus shows us what God is like, and the word is *love*. God is not a powermonger, demanding his "pound of flesh," but rather a loving father, a father who cares, a father who understands, a faithful father, concerned about the welfare of his children.

It is interesting to note how often Jesus said, "Fear not," "Don't be afraid," or "Fret no more." It is also interesting to note in the Christmas story in Luke's Gospel, the first thing the angel says to the shepherds: "Do not be afraid."

This is the most significant gift of Christmas! God gives us a new understanding of what God is like, a new experience of God's compassion and tenderness; a new relationship with God — a relationship built not of fear, but of love. You see, every now and then, Christmas breaks into the wild confusion and reminds us that God is a loving God, and that's what keeps us going.

Every Now and Then, Christmas Breaks Through and Clears Up Our Confusion About Other People — and How We Should Relate to Them

Christmas clears up our ethical confusion. Christmas gives us a new respect and regard for others. Every now and then, Christmas breaks through the fog and *really* shows us that people are more important than things, that people are not pawns to be used and manipulated, but *persons* to be loved and appreciated. Christmas reminds us that we are family.

In one "Peanuts" comic strip, Charlie Brown and Linus are watching television. Snoopy is standing on top of the TV set, his ears stuck up in a V shape. He is serving as the antenna.

Then Charlie Brown says to Linus, "I don't understand it either. All I know is that he gives us a better picture!"

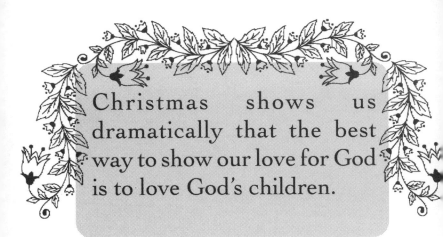

Christmas shows us dramatically that the best way to show our love for God is to love God's children.

I confess that I don't understand everything about the coming of the Christ Child. All I know is that He gives us a better picture. He sharpens the image. He clears up the confusion a bit and shows us not only what God is like, but what God wants us to be like. Christmas shows us dramatically that the best way to show our love for God is to love God's children.

Some years ago, a letter came to our home that moved me as much as any letter I have ever read. It was from a friend named Wanda. She had invited me to her church to speak at a special Christmas program early in December. Because of the hectic pace of the Christmas rush, I really didn't think I should go, but because of my appreciation for Wanda, I accepted and went.

Two days later, the letter came. It was a letter from Wanda. But it was not addressed to me! It was addressed to our children, Jodi and Jeff. They were six and nine at the time. Here is part of the letter:

Dear Jodi and Jeff,

I know most of the mail that comes to your house goes to your mom and dad, so I wanted to write to you. I am writing to thank you for sharing your dad with our community. You are so nice to share him with others, and I want you to know that I appreciate it.

Love, Wanda

When the children let me see the letter, my eyes filled with tears, because I was so touched by her thoughtfulness — much more than I would have been, had the letter been written to me. She wrote to our children, and that touched me!

Then it broke through to me. That's what Christmas is really all about! Love for the children is the best way to show love for God. If you want to express your love and appreciation to God, the best way to do it is to love God's children.

This is what the prophets meant when they said that God doesn't care about burnt offerings, or sacrifices, or lavish prayers. What God really wants is for us to be merciful, kind, forgiving, thoughtful, and loving toward one another. That's why Christ came — to show us how to care, to teach us how to love, to remind us that we are family.

That's the "good news" of Christmas, and every now and then, we experience others as family, and that's what keeps us going.

Every Now and Then, Christmas Breaks Through and Clears Up Our Confusion About Values, About What Is Really Important

Christmas clears up our confusion about priorities. Let me share a true story that happened several years ago.

Jack Smith had been asked by his church to do one of the Christmas Social Concerns projects. He was assigned to take two little boys from a poor home on a Christmas Eve shopping spree. Tommy (age nine), and his younger brother, Billy (age seven), were delighted when Jack Smith came from the church to pick them up. They had been watching for him all morning, with great excitement, because their dad was out of work, and they knew that this was all the Christmas they would have this year.

Jack Smith gave them the allotted $4.00 each, and they started out. Jack took them first to a toy store, but strangely, Tommy and Billy didn't seem too interested. Jack Smith made suggestions, but always their answer was a solemn shake of the head, no.

Then they tried a hobby shop with the same results. Then a candy store, and later, a sporting-goods store. They even tried a boys clothing store, but no luck. Tommy and Billy would whisper to each other and look at a piece of brown wrapping paper they were carrying, but nothing yet had struck their fancy.

Finally, Jack Smith asked, "Where would you boys like to look next?" Their faces brightened. This was the moment they had been waiting for.

"Could we go to a shoe store, sir?" asked nine-year-old Tommy. "We really want to get a pair of shoes for our daddy, so he can go to work."

In the shoe store, the clerk asked what the boys wanted. Out came the brown paper. "We want a pair of work shoes to fit this foot," they said.

Billy explained that it was the outline of their daddy's foot, drawn with a crayon. They had drawn it while their father was asleep in a chair. The clerk measured the outline of the foot and found some shoes that would fit.

"Will these do?" he asked. The boys were delighted. Billy and Tommy, with big smiles, accepted the shoes eagerly.

But then Tommy saw the price. "Oh, no! Billy! These shoes are $16.95, and we have only $8.00."

The clerk cleared his throat and said, "Well, that's the regular price, but you're in luck. It just so happens that those shoes are on sale today—today only, for $3.98."

Then, with the shoes happily in hand, Tommy and Billy bought gifts for their mother and two little sisters. Not once did they think of themselves. The day after Christmas, Jack Smith saw their father out on the street looking for a job. He had the new shoes on his feet and gratitude in his eyes.

He said to Jack, "I thank God for people like you who care!"

Jack Smith answered, "I thank God for your two boys. They taught me more about Christmas in one day than I had learned in a lifetime." (New York: Guideposts [*Guideposts Christmas Treasury,* 1972], p. 202).

Every now and then, Christmas reminds us of what is really important in life, and we realize that our list of priorities needs readjusting! We experience the joy of selfless giving, and that's what keeps us going.

Christmas? Or confusion? Which will we choose this year? Well, the truth is that we don't have to choose, because Bethlehem always happens in the midst of Bedlam!

Christmas Comes Once Again

"For God so loved the world that he gave his only Son, so that everyone who believes in him may not perish but may have eternal life."

John 3:16

*C*hristmas is a time for the telling of stories. Wonderful, heart-warming stories cluster beautifully around Christmas. Here is one of my favorites. It's called "The Gift of a Child," and it was written by M. A. Matthews for the *Guideposts Christmas Treasury*:

The day was frightfully cold, with swirls of snow in the air, and I was looking out the living room window which faces our church. Workmen had just finished constructing the annual nativity scene in the churchyard when school let out for the day. Children gathered excitedly around the crèche, but they didn't stay long; it was far too cold for lingering. All the children (took a quick look at the manger scene and then) hurried away—except for a tiny girl of about six.

The wind lashed at her bare legs and caused her coat to fly open in the front, but she was oblivious of the weather. (She was captivated by that manger scene.) All her attention was riveted on the statues before her. Which one, I couldn't tell. Was it Mary? The baby? The shepherds? The wise men? The animals? I wondered!

And then (a beautiful and poignant moment), I saw her remove her blue woolen head scarf. The wind quickly knotted her hair into a wild tangle, but she didn't seem to notice that either. She had only one thought. Lovingly, she wrapped her scarf around the statue of the baby Jesus. After she had covered it, she patted the baby, and then kissed him on the cheek. Satisfied, she skipped on down the street, her hair frosted with tiny diamonds of ice. As I watched that, I realized that *Christmas had come once again.* (New York: Guideposts [*The Guideposts Christmas Treasury,* 1972], p. 201)

> Christmas is more than poinsettias and presents and parades and pageants, nice as those are. So what really makes Christmas happen for us?

That touching little story raises a good question that we need to think about: "How does Christmas really come for us?" Christmas is more than a date on a calendar. It is more than a vague annual nod in the direction of Bethlehem. Christmas is more than poinsettias and presents and parades and pageants, nice as those are. So what really makes Christmas happen for us? What puts the meaning of Christmas deep in our souls and writes the Christmas Spirit indelibly on our hearts?

Of course, the essence of Christmas is *love*. God's incredible love for us, as he sends his only Son into the world to save us. So the answer is found here. Whenever and wherever we receive God's sacrificial love, and whenever and wherever we pass it on to others — whenever God's love is accepted and shared — Christmas comes once again. Let me bring this closer to home with three examples.

When We Love God, Christmas Comes Once Again

Mark Trotter, a pastor and a friend of mine, tells about an uncomfortable experience in a church he served some years ago. A certain man was unusually loud, coarse, boisterous, and overbearing, and on many occasions he had embarrassed Mark in public. Every time he saw Mark, in crowded cafeterias, in busy hotel lobbies, in noisy sports arenas, in congested supermarkets, in quiet libraries, and even in elegant restaurants, the man would shout out, "Here comes the man of God! Attention, everybody! Here he comes — the man of God! Look, everybody! The man of God is here!"

Now, Mark is a bit shy and reserved, and this man's booming voice, of course, always embarrassed him. Let me hurry to say that Mark is not ashamed of being a Christian or of being a minister, but the way the man would so blatantly point him out was disconcerting, to say the least. Mark said he sort of felt like Clark Kent with his cover blown!

But then one day, after embarrassing Mark again, the man spoke directly to him: "So, how is the man of God today?"

"Just fine, thank you," came the reply. Then Mark added, "By the way, whose man are you?"

The boisterous man was silent. He didn't know what to say. He probably didn't like the question, and he may have detected a little irritation in it. But if we stop to think about it, the question is a good one: By the way, whose man are you? Whose woman are you? Whose child? Whose person? Whose disciple?

One of the best-known and most beloved verses in the Bible is John 3:16: "For God so loved the world that he gave his only Son, that everyone who believes in him may not perish, but may have eternal life." That's what Christmas is really all about. We needed a Savior, and God sent us one. We needed a Messiah, and God sent us one. We needed a Christ, and God sent us one. God so loved the world that he gave the world his only Son.

> When we, like the shepherds of old, fall down in awe, wonder, and commitment before the manger of God's love, Christmas comes once again.

When we, like the shepherds of old, fall down in awe, wonder, and commitment before the manger of God's love, Christmas comes once again. When we, like the wise men, give our best to the Master, Christmas comes once again. When we, like Mary and Joseph, trust God and obey God and try our best to do God's will, Christmas comes once again.

When we accept God's love, when we receive the Messiah into our hearts and commit our lives in faith to him, whenever and wherever that happens, Christmas comes once again. That's the starting place. When we feel God's love and accept God's love and respond to God's love and return God's love and commit to God's love, Christmas comes once again.

When We Love Our Families, Christmas Comes Once Again

From that very first silent and holy night long ago in Bethlehem, Christmas has been a family matter. Just as the shepherds of old were drawn to the stable, at Christmastime today, we are drawn toward home. There is a longing to go home for Christmas, to be with our families. Unfortunately, however, in many homes this Christmas, there will be a chill in the air. You see, there is a big difference between everybody being at home and being at home with everybody.

Sadly, in some families there is estrangement, alienation, division, uneasiness, tension, bitterness, hostility—made all the more graphic by the sanctity of the Christmas season. And that is so pathetic, so sad, so tragic. How many people will be injured or killed this Christmas because of a family member's anger? How many squabbles will break out? How many obscenities will be screamed? How many embarrassing scenes will unfold this Christmas, because some family members can't get along?

A few years ago, just after Christmas, a young college student came to see me. I could tell immediately that she was so happy. Her face was radiant, glowing with joy.

"We had the best Christmas ever," she said.

"Oh, you got some nice presents, did you?" I responded.

"Well," she said, "I did receive some wonderful gifts, but that wasn't it. That wasn't what made this Christmas so special."

She paused for a moment and then went on, "Jim, I'm twenty years old now. I have been on this earth for twenty years. And for the first time in my life, for the first time in twenty years, Mom and Dad didn't get into a big fight at Christmas this year! It was the best Christmas we ever had!"

Whenever and wherever there is peace and harmony and tenderness and respect and thoughtfulness and caring in the family, Christmas comes once again.

When We Love Other People, Christmas Comes Once Again

Many years ago, there lived in a small village a cobbler by the name of Conrad. Dad by day, early and late, the "tap, tap, tap" of his hammer could be heard as he mended the shoes brought to him by the villagers. Though alone and poor, this kindly older man always had a warm and friendly word for everyone, and many folks took lighter hearts, as well as their carefully mended shoes, away from his hut.

Christmas is a time when families draw close together, but for Conrad, there was no one to look forward to with joy. He had no family with whom he could share his Christmas. On Christmas morning, some neighbors, thinking how alone he was, decided to pay him a visit. They found him sweeping away the snow in front of his home and, to their surprise, his face was radiant and happy as he greeted them.

As they entered his house, they gazed in amazement. Instead of a dreary room, they saw a place made festive with holly and evergreen. Christmas decorations brightened the walls and hung gracefully from the rafters. And the table was set for two. Obviously, Conrad was expecting a guest.

"Last night," Conrad said, "the Lord himself appeared to me in a dream, and he told me that I would not be alone on Christmas Day, for he himself was coming to be my guest. That is why I have prepared so joyfully. Everything is ready now. I am waiting for him to come."

When we see Christ in other people and love them, Christmas comes once again.

After the neighbors left, Conrad sat by the window, quietly watching and waiting for the Lord to come. As he watched, the minutes passed into hours, but he scarcely noticed because he was so excited. While he watched, a beggar passed his window — ragged, weary, almost frozen in the harsh winter winds. Conrad called him in. He offered him the warmth of his humble home and gave him some shoes for his frozen feet.

After the beggar left, an old woman hobbled by, carrying on her back a heavy load of firewood. Conrad ran out, lifted the load from her back, and helped her into his little home. There he gave her some food for her starved body, and after she had rested a bit, he helped her on her way again.

Again, Conrad positioned himself by the window to watch and wait for his Lord. But now he heard the sound of a child sobbing. When Conrad opened his front door, he found a small child wandering in the snow, lost and frightened. Some warm milk and soothing words stilled the frightened cries, and soon afterward, Conrad restored the lost child to its mother's arms.

Once more Conrad returned to his vigil. But now the sun was sinking, and the wintry Christmas Day was coming to an end.

But where was his promised guest? Anxious and weary and somewhat disappointed, Conrad dropped to his knees and prayed: "O Lord, what delayed you?"

Broken-hearted, he pleaded, "Lord, what happened? I waited and watched for you all day. Why didn't you come? Why didn't you come?"

Then out of the silence came a beautiful voice: "O Conrad, my Conrad. Don't be dismayed. This very day, three times I came to your friendly door. Three times my shadow crossed your floor. I was a beggar with frozen feet. I was the woman you gave food to eat, and I was the child in the homeless street."

The message of this story is a big part of the message of Christmas, the message of Jesus: "Inasmuch as you

did it unto one of the least of these, you did it unto me."
When we see Christ in other people and love them,
then at that precise moment, Christmas comes once
again. When we love God, when we love our families,
when we love other people, there is Christmas!

8
Keeping Christmas

An angel of the Lord appeared to him in a dream, saying, "Joseph, son of David, do not fear to take Mary your wife, for that which is conceived in her is of the Holy Spirit; she will bear a son, and you shall call his name Jesus, for he will save his people from their sins."

Matthew 1:20-21 RSV

We have trouble "keeping Christmas." In other words, we have trouble sustaining the Spirit of Christmas after the festivities are over. It gets away from us. Too quickly, it slips through our fingers.

Some years ago, when Lou Holtz was the head coach of the Arkansas Razorback football team, he was taking his team to play a bowl game in

Tempe, Arizona. The game was to be played on Christmas Day. He was asked how he felt about playing a football game on Christmas, instead of being at home with his family.

Lou Holtz answered candidly, "Frankly, I'd rather be in Tempe. After all, once you've been to church, had Christmas dinner, and opened the gifts, Christmas is the most boring day of the year."

Coach Holtz was expressing what many people feel—that sinking emptiness, that emotional letdown, that mellow sadness of Christmas afternoon, which makes us wonder, "Where did the spirit of Christmas go? How could we have lost it so quickly?"

Consider these vignettes that underscore the problem: First, a letter to Santa, written by a middle-aged woman.

Dear Santa:

It has been a long, long time since I have written to you. I have now moved from the old home on Happy Street to a house of loneliness and doubt which stands at the end of Disillusion Avenue. All the gloriously bright little baubles that I had in years gone by are now either broken or tarnished and tear-stained. Please bring me a few of those precious toys that I once had—the shining bubbles of joy; the tinkling bells of cheer that rang in my voice; the candles of faith that shone in my eyes; the frankincense and myrrh of steadfast hope that strengthened my soul; and the lode star of universal love that gleamed in my heart.

I realize now that I did not appreciate those priceless treasures in the years past. I did not care for them as I should have. I let them slip away. But now I repent my carelessness. So I will hang my empty heart by the chimney, and humbly ask you to please bring me another supply of Christmas.

Here we have the rather poignant expression of a woman who has realized sadly that somehow, somewhere along the way, she lost Christmas.

Second, there is a "Dennis the Menace" cartoon that the newspapers run almost every year: It's Christmas afternoon, and Dennis has finally opened all his presents; he is up to his chin in wall-to-wall toys. You can't see the floor for all his presents. The caption is a lament. Dennis says, "Is this all?"

How can we hold on to the spirit of Christmas? How can we make Christmas last all year? Some years ago, I got a clue to the answer. I thought I had heard of everything, but this was a new one on me. I came in from work one Monday evening to discover my family giving our Christmas tree a baby aspirin. They had read that when you water your Christmas tree, if you will also toss in a baby aspirin, it will cause your tree to last longer, to stay fresh longer.

> Maybe we have concentrated so much on the gifts we give to one another that we have missed the gifts Christmas gives to us.

I'm sure that is true, because we are doing it again this year, as we've done every year, but I am also sure that our tree will soon give up the ghost. No matter how many aspirins, no matter how much water, no matter how much tender care we give the tree, it won't last forever. It will wilt and dry up; it will wither and die! Why? Because it has been cut off from its roots!

Maybe that's our problem, when it comes to keeping Christmas. Maybe we have trouble making Christmas last, keeping Christmas fresh, because we have lost our roots. Maybe our celebration of Christmas is not rooted deeply enough. Maybe we have concentrated so much on the gifts we give to one another that we have missed the gifts Christmas gives to us.

Christmas has some very special gifts for you and me. The Christ Child celebrates his birthday by giving gifts to those he loves, and in those gifts lie the deep roots of what Christmas is really all about.

I heard about a wealthy couple who had gone on vacation to Hawaii. The husband went out to the beach one afternoon to discover that his wife had just been rescued from the surf and was being revived by the lifeguards.

"What are you doing?" he asked.

The lifeguards replied, "We are giving her artificial respiration."

"Artificial nothing," he shouted. "Give her the real thing. We can afford it!"

Well, we can afford the real root message of Christmas. Matthew's story is helpful. We see here that the Christ Child gives us three special Christmas gifts. And as we've already seen, they are three of the most important gifts that we can pass along to others.

The Christ Child Gives Us Truth

In Matthew, we read that "the child is of the Holy Spirit." What does that phrase mean? Over that phrase, much ink has been spilled and many words spoken. But for the moment, let's concentrate on the great truth here, as Matthew would wish us to do—indeed, as God would wish us to do.

In Jewish thought, the Holy Spirit was the truth giver. The Holy Spirit was the way God's truth was brought to

God's people. It was the Holy Spirit who taught the prophets what to say; it was the Holy Spirit who taught the people of God what to do; it was the Holy Spirit who, down through the ages, brought God's truth to the world. So when Matthew says, "The child . . . is from the Holy Spirit," he is really saying, "Here he is—the truth giver. Here it is—God's truth wrapped up in a person—this baby is of God."

If you want to know what God is like, look at Jesus. If you want to be what God wants you to be, then be like Jesus. This is the Christ Child's Christmas gift to us—the gift of truth.

The Christ Child Gives Us Hope

When Matthew tries to tell us what the Christ event is really all about, he very wisely reaches back into the Old Testament and pulls out an old word, dusts it off, and uses it: *Emmanuel.*

Matthew sums up the message of Christmas in one word: Emmanuel, which means "God with us." And it also means that God is for us. It means that God is on our side, God will not desert us. That is our hope. Nothing can separate us from God and his watchful care. Nothing! Not even death!

On a Monday morning some years ago, I had a long distance call from a dear friend. She said, "I'm thinking of you especially today." I knew what she meant. It was December 17. Some years before on that day, my mother had died in a car wreck. It is difficult to lose a loved one at Christmas time, but the message of Christmas keeps us going.

Emmanuel—God is with us, and nothing, not even death, can separate us from God. That, too, is the Christ Child's gift to us—the gift of hope.

The Christ Child Gives Us Love

"Love came down at Christmas." That's the way the hymn writer puts it. This is the root message of Christmas—that God is love, and God wants us to be loving. To paraphrase First John, "Whoever loves is a child of God and a child of Christmas." Henry Van Dyke put it this way:

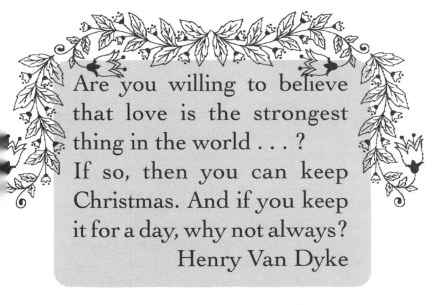

Are you willing to believe that love is the strongest thing in the world . . . ?
If so, then you can keep Christmas. And if you keep it for a day, why not always?
Henry Van Dyke

There is a better thing than the observance of Christmas Day, and that is keeping Christmas. Are you willing to believe that love is the strongest thing in the world, stronger than hate, stronger than evil, stronger than death, and that the blessed life which began in Bethlehem nineteen hundred years ago is the image and brightness of the Eternal Love? If so, then you can keep Christmas. And if you keep it for a day, why not always?

I received a letter from a young woman who recently joined our church. I first met her when I spoke to an Alcoholics Anonymous group. She was a teenage alcoholic, but she has not had a drink in several years. She has since found a home in the church, a community of love. She has graciously permitted me to share a portion of what she wrote:

Dear Jim:

In this beautiful time of Advent and Christmas, I'd like to say thank you for being in our club that Thursday night. I decided that night to try this church, and thank God for that! My life has definitely found meaning and direction in the past three months. I found a group of people who were real, and who accepted me for who I am. The love and concern of one person for another is so beautiful! And now I can say the name *Jesus* without flinching, and I'm learning how to love him without feeling fanatical. My whole concept of God is changing from fear to love.

My daughter has benefited so much too. She loves

the nursery and told me last Sunday that it's "Happy Birthday Jesus" time. I can't think of a better way to rear a child.

Thank all of you so very much for what the church is meaning to me. May God bless you and your family, and may you be filled with the peace and love of Christmas forever, one day at a time.

Isn't that a great letter? And isn't that what Christmas is about? It's about caring, accepting, and loving people. It's about truth and hope and love. When we grab those things and make them a part of our lives, we can really keep Christmas, and we can celebrate with great joy the Christmas gifts that always fit.

9
Christmas Memories

"Indeed, God did not send the Son into the world to condemn the world, but in order that the world might be saved through him."

John 3:17

*I*f you were to write down your favorite Christmas memory, what would it be? Would it be the memory of your mother baking Christmas cookies in the kitchen, or your dad making a stand for the Christmas tree? Would it be the beautiful sound of a favorite Christmas carol, or the distinctive fragrance of Christmas ever-greens in your home?

Would it be the memory of a live manger scene, or your first kiss under the mistletoe? Would it be a special present you received, or one you gave? Would it be the memory of celebrating Christmas Eve communion at church, or hearing Granddad read Luke's Christmas story to the family as you gathered in front of the fireplace?

Would it be the remembrance of Christmas in a foreign land—a year when you could not get home for the holidays? Or would it be the memory of a great choir singing the "Hallelujah!" chorus from *Messiah* in a majestic concert in a beautiful sanctuary, or of young carolers singing "Silent Night" off-key at your front door?

> Christmas evokes powerful memories. . . . That's why we celebrate it—to remind us about God and his incredible concern for us.

I remember one Christmas when I was pretty young. My brother and sister and I announced that we would make all the ornaments for the tree, that we would decorate the tree from top to bottom with only our homemade ornaments. We made the decorations with paper, pictures, candy, popcorn, and cranberries. And when we were through, an outsider would have been underwhelmed by the sight of that tree. But our parents thought it was (without question) the most beautiful Christmas tree they had ever seen!

We need Christmas . . . to wake us up, to bring us back, to jog our memories, to remind us again of what this life is all about.

Christmas memories—no other season, no other time of the year, touches our hearts quite like Christmas. You know, when you stop to think about it, memory is indeed a wonderful gift that God has given us. It's the way we learn, it's the way we celebrate, and (as amnesia so dramatically demonstrates) it is absolutely crucial for our sense of personal identity. Our forbears in the faith were vividly aware of the importance of memory. That's why we have seasons and traditions, and festivals and symbols and colors and special days — to remind us of who we are and whose we are!

> Deep down inside — deeper than some of us even realize — we all relate to Ebenezer Scrooge. We all need to be converted from selfishness to love.

Christmas evokes powerful memories — and with good reason. That's precisely what it's supposed to do!

That's what it's designed to do! That's why we celebrate it—to remind us about God and his incredible concern for us, to remind us about the real priorities of life—love, joy, peace, justice, forgiveness. It reminds us of the importance of family, friends, and church, of what God is like and what God wants us to be like. Christmas reminds us of the things that really matter.

Hannah Moore once wrote: "The world does not require so much to be informed as reminded." Well, how is your memory? Do you have a good memory? Most of us confess that we don't. Several years ago, I took a memory course, and after the final session, they gave us a booklet designed to help us reinforce, internalize, and implement all the good things we had learned in that course to improve our memories. I'm sure that booklet on memory would be a great help to me, but I can't for the life of me remember where I put it!

That's why we need Christmas—to wake us up, to bring us back, to jog our memories, to remind us again of what this life is all about. With that in mind, let me underscore three things that Christmas reminds us of.

Christmas Reminds Us That We Need a Savior

Literally, the name *Jesus* means "The Lord is Salvation," "Yahweh Saves," or "Savior." Jesus came at Christmas to do for us what we cannot do for ourselves. He came to save us from our sins.

Outside of the Bible, the most famous Christmas story ever written is *A Christmas Carol* by Charles Dickens. Dickens' story is about a gruff, miserly character named Ebenezer Scrooge and a little crippled boy named Tiny Tim Cratchit, who is always saying, "God Bless Us, Every One!" Actually, it's a story about conversion. And did Scrooge ever need converting! I mean, he was a despicable character—a selfish, arrogant, hardhearted, mean-spirited, uncaring, unsympathetic, unchristian tightwad. His now famous response to Christmas, "Bah! Humbug!" has become the sad symbol of his sick spirit.

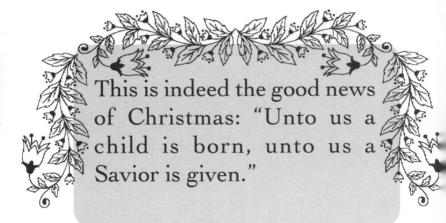

This is indeed the good news of Christmas: "Unto us a child is born, unto us a Savior is given."

As the story unfolds, Ebenezer Scrooge is visited one night by some ghosts who subject him to a haunting, the likes of which few characters in fiction have experienced. Frightened by the ghosts, Scrooge is forced to see himself as he really is. The visits of the ghosts and the Christlike unconditional love of the Cratchit family (who keep on loving him, even though he has treated them horribly) combine to convert Ebenezer Scrooge. And now, with a second chance, he changes completely! A skinflint no more, he becomes an everloving grandfather type. He loves Christmas now. He gets into the spirit of the season, sending presents to the Cratchits and a large amount of money to charity. He dresses up and goes to his nephew's house for Christmas dinner. And he announces that he is giving his clerk, Bob Cratchit, a nice raise.

Why are we so fascinated with this story? It's not just that it's a well-written classic piece of literature. There is something more here. This is our story. Deep down inside — deeper than some of us even realize — we all relate to Ebenezer Scrooge. We all need help. We all have our clay feet. We all need to face up to ourselves. We all need to be converted from selfishness to love. We all need a Savior.

Two thousand years ago, God looked down and saw the sick, Scrooge-like spirit of the world, and God knew the world would not work that way. So God's Son was sent to save us, and change us, and show us a better way. Once a year, Christmas comes around again to jog our memories, to remind us how much we need a Savior.

Christmas Reminds Us That We Have a Savior

I have a friend who was a prisoner of war in Vietnam for more than two years. It was an indescribably horrendous, dehumanizing experience, and only his deep faith enabled him to survive. He told me that through that long, horrible period as a P.O.W. in Vietnam, the one thing that saved him, that saved his health and sanity, was the strong sense of Christ's presence with him. He said that the enemy could take away his freedom, they could take away his fellow Americans, they could take away his food and his dignity. But the one thing they couldn't take away from him was his Savior—that strong sense of Christ's presence with him.

> Every time we reach out to help others in the spirit of Christ . . . we are sharing the Savior. We are living in the spirit of Christmas.

He said, "Death called to me from every direction. It was in the air I breathed, but somehow I was serene and confident, because I knew Christ was with me. And even if death came, he would be there with me too!" He said, "I kept remembering how Paul put it: 'Nothing, not even death, can separate us from God and his love!' "

This is the good news of our faith, isn't it? This is indeed the good news of Christmas: "Unto us a child is born, unto us a Savior is given." No matter in what circumstances we find ourselves, we can count on that. Christmas reminds us that we need a Savior, and we have one!

Christmas Reminds Us That We Can Share the Savior

The Christ Child comes at Christmas to show us what God is like and what God wants us to be like — and the world is Love. Every time we show love for another person, we are living in the spirit of Christ, we are sharing the Savior, we are keeping alive the power of Christmas.

I'm a fan of the "Peanuts" comic strip. One of my favorites is one where Lucy decides that Linus (her little brother) has to grow up and learn to live without his security blanket. So when Linus falls asleep, she slips the blanket out of his hands, takes it outside, and buries it. When Linus wakes up and discovers his blanket is missing, he panics and falls to the floor. He can't get his breath! He gasps and screams, "I've got to have that blanket. I can't live without my blanket."

Then Snoopy sees Linus's dilemma and rises to the occasion. He goes outside and, with his trusty nose, sniffs out the blanket, digs it up, and brings it back to Linus. Linus is so relieved. With one arm, he grabs the blanket, and with the other, he hugs Snoopy, saying, "Oh thank you, thank you, Snoopy. You have saved my life!" The last picture shows Snoopy lying on his back on top of his doghouse, looking contented, and thinking "Every now and then my existence is justified!"

Love is indeed the justification of our existence. Every time we reach out to help others in the spirit of Christ, every time we show kindness in the spirit of Christ, every time we express love in the spirit of Christ, we are sharing the Savior. We are living in the spirit of Christmas.

Christmas memories—there are so many that touch our hearts and warm our souls. This year, I hope and pray that above all else, we will remember these three. We need a Savior! We have a Savior! We can share the Savior!